Making
the Sale

The Lessons Learned Series

Wondering how the most accomplished leaders from around the globe have tackled their toughest challenges? Now you can find out—with Lessons Learned. Concise and engaging, each volume in this new series offers twelve to fourteen insightful essays by top leaders in business, the public sector, and academia on the most pressing issues they've faced.

A crucial resource for today's busy executive, Lessons Learned gives you instant access to the wisdom and expertise of the world's most talented leaders.

Other books in the series:

⊰ LESSONS LEARNED ⊱

Making the Sale

LES50NS
Boston, Massachusetts

Library of Congress Cataloging-in-Publication Data

Making the sale.
    p. cm. — (Lessons learned)
  ISBN 978-1-4221-2302-7
  1. Sales management. 2. Selling.
  HF5438.4.M35 2008
  658.85—dc22

                              2007048564

In partnership with Fifty Lessons, a leading provider of digital media content,
Harvard Business School Press is pleased to
announce the launch of Lessons Learned,
a new book series that showcases the trusted
voices of the world's most experienced
leaders. Through the power of personal
storytelling, each book in this series pre-
sents the accumulated wisdom of some of
the world's best-known experts and offers
insights into how these individuals think,
approach new challenges, and use hard-won
lessons from experience to shape their leadership philosophies. Organized thematically
according to the topics at the top of managers' agendas—leadership, change management, entrepreneurship, innovation, and
strategy, to name a few—each book draws
from Fifty Lessons' extensive video library
of interviews with CEOs and other thought

A Note from the Publisher

leaders. Here, the world's leading senior executives, academics, and business thinkers speak directly and candidly about their triumphs and defeats. Taken together, these powerful stories offer the advice you'll need to take on tomorrow's challenges.

We invite you to join the conversation now. You'll find both new ways of looking at the world, and the tried-and-true advice you need to illuminate the path forward.

⊣ CONTENTS ⊢

Contents

Contents

Making
the Sale

Prove to Your Customers That You Care

Richard Santulli

Founder and CEO, NetJets

WHAT I TELL MY SALESMEN is that they're selling a product that everybody wants and that's unusual. We're probably called the highest-end luxury brand in the world, and we sell stuff that is very expensive. But from a sales point of view, you can be a jewelry salesman and say, "Everybody likes jewelry." Well, maybe a lot of people do; I don't. If you were trying to sell me jewelry, I wouldn't be interested.

But there are not many people in the world who, if you asked, "Would you like to have a private jet and the ability to fly a private jet?" would say, "No, I'd rather not." So I tell my salesmen, "You're selling something that people will want. Now, can they afford it? Are they willing to spend the money? How will it change their life?" Those are the things that my sales professionals have to be able to relate to a customer.

You build a company by leading. And you lead a sales team, basically, by showing how you care about the customers. A very interesting story, which one of the guys on my sales team uses at the beginning of every sales meeting, goes back to 1998. And the reason I know the date you'll find out in a second.

I live in, more or less, southern New Jersey. One of my senior salespeople, Steve Eisman, called and said he was having trouble with a prospective customer who lived in my area and whom I didn't know.

But I was a pretty well-known person in the area. I had just moved into the area about two years before. The reason my salesman was having so much difficulty with him was that this potential customer said, "Listen, you guys are so big relative to the competition that you're not going to really care about me." That's what X-Y-Z company, my competitor, was telling him—that he'd be a big deal for my competitor and he wouldn't very much matter to NetJets. So I said to Steve, "Okay, give me his number."

This was on a Saturday, about twelve o'clock. I called him, and I said, "Hello, Ray. I'm Rich Santulli. I know you've been talking to Steve," et cetera. "You seem to be concerned that we don't really care about our customers."

He said, "Yes, Rich. You guys are big and successful, and I'm just a little guy."

I said, "Ray, I'll give you $1 million,"—this is a true story—"if you can guess what I'll be doing in the next hour."

Making the Sale

He said, "Are you serious?"

I said, "Yes, I'll give you $1 million." He made about three guesses. I said, "Ray, as we speak, it's now ten after twelve. I'm getting married at one o'clock at my house. I'm standing on my front lawn, and my wife-to-be is screaming at me to get off the telephone. But I insisted that I give you a call to show you that we do care." He's been my customer since 1998, and a happy one.

That story is basically the way we explain it to our salespeople—you have to show the customer that you care. Because if you don't show the customer that you care, then he's not an important part of your business. That's the way, in my opinion, that my sales team has to act. They have to.

Every customer is important. It doesn't matter whether they buy a sixteenth from us, a quarter from us. You have to make them feel special. And you make them feel special by being special with them. That story still resonates very well today. It's used every time there's a sales conference.

TAKEAWAYS

- When selling, you must relate to your customers, knowing how the products or services will change their lives and whether they will spend money on them.

- To lead a sales team effectively, you have to show that you care about your customers. Lead by example, and go the extra mile.

- Every customer is important, and making customers feel special is simply a matter of spending time with them.

Judgment Calls

Phil Smith

Head of Technology and Corporate Marketing,
Europe, Cisco Systems

JUDGMENT IS THE KEY SKILL for
someone operating in business. Actually,
you may argue that this is the key skill for
people operating in life generally. But it's
certainly something I've seen as a key attribute for success in business.

Judgment is a fairly broad word, but it really
is knowing when to make the right call and

what the right call is, knowing when to do something and not to do something.

I can remember a customer meeting many years ago with a good friend of mine. He's worked in a number of businesses throughout the communication space, but he's probably the best sales guy I've ever worked with. His greatest skill is knowing when to push back to a customer; because typically when you're working with a customer, there's a level of negotiation that goes back and forth regarding what you're offering and the price or the conditions of the customer you want to meet. But there is some point when that has to stop, and you have to say, "Now it's all over."

I remember this particular example very clearly. We were in a meeting where we were right at the eleventh hour on a huge deal that we were trying to close with one of the major banks in the U.K. At this meeting there was a key proponent from the bank who was working with us and who had been the chief negotiator on the deal.

Making the Sale

He raised what was, frankly, a fairly ridiculous objection to what we were doing. It was one of those things that we, as an organization trying to serve, could have risen to and said, "Well, we believe that this particular argument is invalid."

This colleague of mine, who was driving the sales campaign at the time, simply turned around and in not too subtle terms told the person to "cease and desist," shall we say.

That very clearly said, "That's it; it's over." He said it in a fairly shocking way.

Everyone just stopped for a second, looked around, and said, "My God, what have we done? This guy could easily just run off now and say, 'I'm not going to be spoken to like that from a vendor.'"

But, of course, it was exactly the right time because the guy just turned around, smiled, and said, "You're absolutely right. You've done exactly the right thing; right call. That's fine. Let's move on from there."

Making the Sale

There was that judgment call, which was very dangerous in the campaign because this was a $150 million deal for our partner and a $20 million deal for Cisco. It could have been compromised. But his judgment to push back at that moment was absolutely key.

That attribute in sales is very important, but it's also very important in other places. We're all limited on resources; we don't have enough time to do what we're all doing, particularly in a fast-growing business like the one I'm involved in, where there are a million things I could do. I have plenty of areas in my job that I could focus on, everything from community investment right through to technical strategy or M&A activity. But unless you can make the call that says, "At this point, this is the right thing to do," you will never prevail.

TAKEAWAYS

- ⚑ In business, judgment is a key skill for success.

- ⚑ Ultimately, judgment comes down to knowing when to make the right call and knowing what the right call is.

- ⚑ Sometimes the right judgment call requires pushing back on the customer, and you will never succeed unless you are willing to make that call.

To Win Big You Have to Risk Losing Big

Mel Lagomasino

Former Chairman and CEO,
JP Morgan Private Bank

THIS LESSON REALLY is all about advising clients, and it is the result of thirty years of doing it myself. The kind of people we advise are people who are extraordinarily successful, very wealthy individuals—typically

people who have net worth well in excess of
$100 million.

My biggest lesson, which I found over
and over again, was that my best relationships came from those individuals with
whom I took the greatest amount of risk. If
you want to win big and win the trust of
these individuals, you have to be willing to
lose big—and lose the relationship by saying
something to them that they absolutely do
not want to hear and that most people are
not willing to tell them, precisely because
they are so important.

I remember a time when I went to see two
siblings. They were billionaires. They were
in the process of trying to figure out what to
do with the next generation. They had just
inherited from their parents. Their parents
had left everything in a joint structure, so
these two were glued at the hip in everything
that they did, and they each were fighting
for control. And so, by the time I stepped
into the picture as their banker/adviser, they
each had an army of lawyers.

Making the Sale

They were the most important people in their city, and everyone lived off them—whether it was the university that got the biggest grants from them; all of the providers of products where this company that they ran was their biggest customer; and particularly these two law firms, each one representing the other, which basically kept creating paperwork and sending them bills.

I remember my first meeting with these two siblings. In addition to me, there was one sibling and the whole army of lawyers representing that sibling, and on the other side was the other sibling and the whole army of lawyers representing the other sibling. And we went back and forth for about two hours, with all the lawyers taking notes.

Finally, I said, "Time out. You should know that from my perspective, the company I work for, whether you do business with us will not make us or break us, and it certainly won't make or break me. So I'm going to take all the risk here and tell you that there is no way we are going to solve

these issues unless the two of you siblings
start talking to each other without your lawyers. If I were you, I would tell your lawyers
to leave the room now, and let's get down to
brass tacks and the real issue, which is control of this company and how we're going to
deal with this company. Let's have the two of
you look each other in the eye and figure
out how we're going to do this and what the
issues are, because until we have that conversation, the only people who are going to
get rich here are the lawyers."

And there was this silence. I thought for
sure I was going to get fired. And I thought,
"I'm totally cool about getting fired, because
it would be absolutely the wrong thing to
allow these two to continue working the way
that they are working."

The interesting thing is, they looked at
each other, they looked at me, they asked us
all to leave the room, and then they asked
me back into the room. They said, "Nobody
has had the guts to talk to us that way, and
you're right. You really shook us up, and we
really think we have to start from scratch.

Making the Sale

Will you stay with us and help us deal with some of these issues?" They actually sent the lawyers home, and that was the beginning of the beginning.

It was the beginning of the beginning for them, in terms of really being able to figure out how they were going to deal with this huge inheritance, this company that they had to run, and start to set up the governance for generation three. To this day—this was probably fifteen years ago—we are great friends. I talk to them all the time. I talk to the siblings, as well as to their children. The great thing is that they always feel that they can tell me exactly what they're thinking, and they know that I'm going to tell them exactly what I'm thinking. And that is priceless.

I realized it with them—but I have to tell you, there are probably another twenty or twenty-five stories that I can think of— who are the people whom I've taken the risk with, who are always the people you're doing the greatest favor and adding the greatest value to.

Making the Sale

I think that the moral to the story in advising clients is that if you want to win big, if you want to win their trust, then you have to be willing to lose big and lose the relationship. You have to be willing to take the risk and tell them the things that they don't want to hear.

TAKEAWAYS

Your best relationships will come from those customers with whom you are willing to take the greatest risks.

The greatest risk often means telling customers exactly what they don't want to hear.

To earn the client's trust and win big, you must be willing to lose big, which means you must be willing to risk the relationship by being honest.

——◆——

Trust Is the Key to Winning Business

Gill Rider

Director General, Leadership and People Strategy,
Cabinet Office, United Kingdom

——◆——

I BELIEVE THAT TRUST is one of the
most important things in the business
world. I learned this when I was a young
consultant really starting in the world of
essentially selling work to help companies
improve themselves.

Making the Sale

One day I was at home with my husband;
it was Sunday, and we were about to go
out for lunch. The phone rings, and it's a
project team that is getting ready to make a
sales presentation the next morning. They
want me to come in and help. I look disap-
pointed; my husband looks angry. But off I
go to the office.

It turns out that they've realized that they
haven't understood quite what the client
wanted, and because I had a relationship
with the client in a past life, they asked if I'd
phone him and ask him some questions.

I get my address book out and find his
home number, and I call him and ask a few
questions. Two and a half hours later I came
off the phone. He had told me so much
about what they wanted, what the team really
needed to do. I went back and reported it.
They turned the presentation around, and
they won the work.

Afterward I said to him, "Why did you do
that? Why did you really tell me all of those
things?"

He said, "Because I trusted you to do the
right thing for my company."

Making the Sale

It really made me think a lot about trust,
so over the years I've examined what you
need to do to build trust. It's very much
about making sure that you get your ego, or
your self-interest, or your company's self-
interest, out of the way and make sure you
hear from the other person exactly what it is
they need, rather than what you think you
want to give them.

I had the opportunity to sit on the other
side of the table for a period of my life. [I
would] actually see people come in as if I was
the client and present proposals to me. It was
always totally extraordinary to me how little
of the decision was a differentiation about
the competence or the credentials, because
generally speaking, once you get to the point
of presenting something and selling something, most of the organizations that have
been invited to that table have the same
credibility and competence. What tends to
come over is, "Do I want to work with these
people? Would I trust these people with the
piece of work that I'm about to give them?"

Ultimately, I think that trust in business
relationships is completely key to getting

work, winning work, and being successful in the business world. And that trust comes from two human beings connecting, on a personal level as well as a professional level.

TAKEAWAYS

⚞ To build trust, you must set aside your interests and those of your company so that you can hear what customers need, not what you want to give them.

⚞ Decision making often comes down to two questions: Do I want to work with these people? Would I trust these people?

⚞ Trust in business is key to being successful and comes from the ability of people to connect on both the personal and the professional level.

Be Persistent

Sir David Michels

Former Group Chief Executive, Hilton

PERSISTENCE—or as my wife calls it, nagging, although *persistence* is the commercial word for this—is an enormously useful tool in business. And it really doesn't matter if it is persistence or nagging, because you use them both to achieve the same end.

I think the single best example I've come across personally of this was when I used to be a salesman for a hotel company called Grand Metropolitan Hotels, which very

unwisely built a hotel called The Britannia
in Grosvenor Square.

I think a committee got together and decided that the hotel was going to have three
hundred single rooms and one hundred
twin rooms [having two beds]. No hotel
anywhere today is built with single rooms
because of the logic: you can get two people
in a twin room and one person in a twin,
but you can't get two people in a single
room. But we decided on three hundred
singles, so on any night we had about two
hundred fifty rooms we could not sell.

In the whole of London at that time,
there was one business that could fill one
hundred seventy of these rooms every single
night, three hundred sixty-five nights a
year. It was called Japan Airlines, which flew
a lot of planes in those days. There was no
competition about. It flew eight or nine
planes into London; so there was the crew.
In those days the unions enforced that they
were held over for three or four days, so you
had three or four days multiplied by [the

number of] crew, multiplied by eight or nine planes.

I was a senior salesman at that time and was basically charged with getting the Japan Airlines crew contract, which I think was at the Royal Lancaster in those days. Both of these hotels still exist.

The Japanese are careful people. They do not make up their minds quickly. They were perfectly well treated by the other hotel, and getting the crew [contract] was, from memory, a two-and-a-half year job. I learned some Japanese; I went to Japan about ten times. I actually took up golf, a game I detest and was terrible at, and because I couldn't afford to belong to a golf club, I took the chief decision maker eight or nine times to my father-in-law's golf club, where everybody was bribed a couple of quid to say, "Hello, David, how are you?" It actually worked, and we just persisted and persisted, waiting for the Royal Lancaster to make a mistake.

One day, after about two years, the Royal Lancaster booked out—overbooked, in

other words—about fifty or sixty of the crew
arriving that day. That was our opening. To
cut a two-and-a-half year story of absolutely
monthly persistence short, the crew decided
to come to the Britannia. We got the contract, and we kept it for about seven years.
The main decision maker and myself became great friends in the end.

It must have been worth £8 or £9 million
in today's money, and the best thing about it
was that, at that time, I had a mad French
managing director called Eric Bernard,
who went on to become chief executive of
Holiday Inn in Memphis. He was a wonderful man. He kissed me on both cheeks—
which for me, as a young Englishman in the
1970s, was a little embarrassing—and promoted me to the board.

I'm not suggesting there was any justice in
that, and I bypassed an awful lot of more
worthy people. But it was so good for the
company that two-and-half years' work,
which could well have ended in failure, by a
bit of luck and by someone else's mistake
ended in success and really paid off.

Making the Sale

In getting any big deal, the first thing you have to do is want it. I know this sounds ridiculous, but you have to dream it and you have to want it. It's like if you're a golfer, you want to be scratch. You're never going to be scratch unless you really, really know it in your heart—not in your mind, because your mind's going to tell you, "I can't get this." Your heart's going to tell you, "I want this." Then the two compete with each other—at least mine do constantly. You really, really have to want it. The most single important thing is wanting it.

If you want something badly enough, you're going to learn everything about it. You're going to play golf even if you don't want to. You're going to really try and learn a little bit of a language and customs that don't come naturally to you, and you're going to do one thing that is probably the most important part of all: you're going to take a risk. Because if you've spent a thousand working hours, let's say, over two-and-a-half years and you fail, you've probably damaged your career a bit and you've probably damaged, in a small way, the company a bit. So you have to be prepared to take the risk.

I often fail. Everyone does, but I certainly do. But I never, ever give in if I have a plan that I think is good for the organization and good for the shareholders. I've had eight-year plans that still haven't come off. I've had one-year plans that have come off, but I see absolutely no reason ever to give in on anything.

TAKEAWAYS

⊣ To land a deal, you must remain persistent.

⊣ You have to know, not only in your mind but also in your heart, "I want this."

Making the Sale

⚔ You must learn along the way, be prepared to do things that come unnatu-
rally, and be prepared to take a risk.

⚔ Ultimately if you want to succeed, you
never, ever give in.

[Handwritten annotations in top margin: "Listen —", "ask the patient, not the doctor", "feedback", ""How'm I doing"", "more & more normal question asked ever"]

Asking Your Customers for Advice

William Ury

Director, Global Negotiation Project

I WAS DOING SOME WORK once with IBM on negotiation. And one of my preferred negotiation techniques is to tell people always to ask the other side—let's say the client—for their advice.

Making the Sale

One day an IBM manager called me up and said, "I've been having a lot of trouble with a deal. It's a $10 million deal. I keep on bringing it to the customer, and the customer, for whatever reason—it's been months now—just won't take it to the board for approval."

He said, "So finally, frustrated, I thought about your idea of asking for advice. I went to the customer, and I said, 'We've been here for six months now. What would you do if you were in my shoes?' In other words, give me some advice about how we can advance this deal. And the customer was a little bit surprised because he's never been asked for his advice before by a salesperson. And [the customer] said, 'I guess if I were in your shoes, I would reframe the deal a little bit this way, or that way, because that might make it easier.'"

[The IBM manager] then said, "By the end of the hour, we were able to reframe the deal so the fellow was willing to take it back to the board and got the agreement, and it wasn't a shift for us in any way in terms of profit."

The advantage of thinking in terms of a negotiation is, you're not just selling but asking the customer for advice. What would you do if you were in their shoes? People like to be asked for their advice; it's respectful. And then they get into it, so suddenly you're two together trying to figure out how you're going to get the deal done in a way that works for the customer, because it's advice about how you can best meet their needs. That's the key in negotiation. You want to meet the customer's needs, and you have to get the customer's help in doing that.

I think the tendency when we go into a sale is that we're always thinking about our problem—how we are going to make the sale, our bonus, our commission, or whatever. The key in negotiation—probably the single most important skill you need—is to be able to put yourself in the other side's shoes—in this case, in the customer's shoes. Think about it from their perspective. See your job as influencing them from their perspective. After all, negotiation is an exercise in influence; you're trying to change someone's mind. If you're trying to change someone's mind, the first thing you need to know is where their mind is right now.

Don't just start the negotiation from your point of view, of what you need. Start the negotiation from their point of view and what they need, and then work back toward a solution that meets your needs as well.

TAKEAWAYS

- When selling, ask the people on the other side for their advice.

- Think about the negotiation from the customer's perspective, and see your job as influencing him from his perspective.

Making the Sale

🎴 To change a customer's mind, you
   need to know where her mind is and
   what she needs, and then you can work
   back toward a solution that meets your
   needs, too.

———◆———

The Person
on the Ground
Knows Best

———◆———

Sir Richard Evans

Chairman, United Utilities

IT'S AN INTERESTING FACT in all businesses that the guys at the top don't always know best. Most of the skills and the experience to deal with an issue reside where the issue actually comes from.

Making the Sale

When I was just a young guy, I had been
dispatched to conclude what, at that time,
was a very big overseas contract in India.
And as anybody will know who's ever been to
India, the government in India is a pretty
bureaucratic organization. But I got into—I
might say, driven by, at that time, the senior
management of the company back in London—quite a contentious argument with
these people, as the potential customer,
over an issue of payments.

It was a very large contract. There were
complex arrangements being negotiated in
order to secure appropriate payments for
the protection of both parties to the contract: the government of India and my company. The guy I was negotiating with was the
senior-most civil servant at that time in the
government. As a part of our standard selling terms, when we had met a particular
milestone we expected to be paid within
thirty days of submitting an invoice.

This guy explained to me that, with the
bureaucracy they had and the processes they

had to go through, there was simply no way they could ever meet a payment on an invoice in less than ninety days. He said, "Look, this isn't a condition of the government's contracting processes. It's simply all the steps we have to go through to get the [needed approvals] from every department that has an involvement in it. It'll take ninety days, and therefore, when you put your invoice in, ninety days later, we'll be able to pay you."

I kept getting instructions from the U.K. end—"No, I'm sorry. We need to be paid in thirty days. And if we don't get paid in thirty days, there are other remedies in the contract. We go into default." The legal ramifications of it got completely out of hand.

Well, this guy convinced me that there was no way they could pay us in less than ninety days. At the end of the day, the guy said, "If you want to put thirty days in there, you put thirty days in. But I'm telling you, you won't get paid for ninety days." So we put thirty days in this contract and eventually signed it. The whole thing turned into a very successful program, but we never, ever got an invoice paid in less than ninety days.

The company itself never would ever have resorted to the legal remedies for what was, technically, a default. And as I grew up in management terms, going into more senior positions, the lesson it taught me was, the guy on the ground actually is the guy who can give you the best advice.

The fact that we had a bunch of lawyers sitting in our head office somewhere saying that you should be able to get paid in thirty days was completely irrelevant. So I've always tried to listen to the guy who's closest to the coalface in dealing with issues. These guys, even though for other reasons you might have cause to not necessarily take their advice, what is damned important is to make sure that when you're looking at the various sort of issues that lie in front of you, you actually know the guy who knows how things work right on the ground floor of the organization. You need to know what he thinks and what he thinks is doable.

If a guy comes in to me and one of the senior managers and says, "This is what I think we should do," I just say, "Who's actually dealing with this?"—well, it can be anybody—"What does he think?" The guys then begin to realize you have to ask them the question, so they go back and make damn sure they know what the guy dealing with the issue actually thinks about it. But I always ask first, "The guy who is dealing with this— what is his view? What is his advice?"

TAKEAWAYS

◄ The people at the top don't always know best. The skill and experience needed to deal with an issue often reside with the people on the front lines.

Making the Sale

- Don't let processes and bureaucracy get in the way of moving forward with a sale.

- Find the person who's closest to the issue, and solicit his advice.

Generating Sales in an Early-Stage Business

David Balter

Founder and CEO, BzzAgent

BzzAgent was an idea that came about in late winter of 2001, and we actually launched as a business in 2002. I'd had some previous businesses that I had sold in late 2001, and I had said, "I don't want to do this again. It's really hard, and I don't know if I can manage." My wife begged me to get a real job, and my parents said to go do something else.

I tried to get a job. No one would hire me. They said, "You're an entrepreneur. You'll never want to work for somebody else," which is not true, but that's what they said. So I started looking for something else to do.

I became obsessed with this idea of word of mouth. I read all the books on the subject and just said, "This is amazing. Nobody has figured out how to organize this into a medium, right? Everyone's talking about the power of these people, the power of communication, but no one's helping a company organize and measure itself." I said, "I'm going to start this business."

There were a couple of things that happened. The first was that there was no money. This was in early 2002. I went out looking for capital. People thought we were being silly. We probably did a hundred capital calls trying to get people to give us some money, and no one would give us money. It was a down economy, and it was hard for people to believe that companies were even worthwhile at this point. It was like, "Oh, you want to start a company. You must be crazy, because, you know, it'll never work out for you."

We found, in a down economy, there was good talent available, and we found a lot of good people to help us try this thing. There were three of us in the beginning. And cheap rent. There were a lot of ways you could use a down economy to help grow a business more quickly.

So we had this idea, and we went out and started talking to agencies. [We said,] "Hey, we have this great idea. You're a creative agency; you service big brands. What if you engaged real consumers and involved them in a campaign where they could talk about your product or service?"

I remember distinctly one massive agency in Boston we went to. This is right around

Making the Sale

May or June of 2002. A friend of a friend
introduced us. We went in, and I sat in this
big room with some senior executives, and I
told him about what we do. It was like a deer
in the headlights. They said, "What are you
talking about? This whole idea seems crazy."
They literally got up, shuffled me out of the
office, and told me not to come back.

This is what it was like in the beginning
for this business, a business that had never
been created before or been done before.
An idea that really flew in the face of a lot of
conventional thinking was a lot of "no." We
heard, "No, I won't buy this." One of the
things we heard a lot of was, "Nobody would
sign up to take part in your service," "No
one would be a consumer who'd want to
volunteer for brands," and "I would never
pay you for it."

As a matter of fact, we finally had to give
the product away for free to get anybody to
buy it. In the end, we went to five companies
and said, "For the last six months, you said
you wouldn't buy this product, so we'll give

it to you for free." Four of those companies said no. They didn't even want it for free. One company, Penguin Publishing, said yes. They said we could work on this book, *The Frog King*. If we were going to do it for free, why not?

We engaged four hundred people to read the book and then tell their friends. In the end the book did its entire year's [worth of] sales in the two months of the campaign. The guy at Penguin—actually pretty smart— said, "That may have worked; it could've just been a good book. Why don't you do it again for a book that's flat-lined for a year? Here's a book I'm going to give you that's done the same amount of sales every month. If you can make that book lift in sales, I'll actually buy a campaign. But this one, again, has to be for free." So we did it again for free, and that book tripled in sales. Now we've done probably forty or fifty books for Penguin over the last five years.

The takeaway here, and this is the thing that I tell any entrepreneur who approaches me or asks what they should do: giving it away for free is not the worst thing in the world. You have to break an idea in somewhere. Case studies are extremely important; they're very valid. You have to try and get somebody who's willing to believe—even if you have to give it away—so you can figure out what to do and how to do it and how to make your product work for a client.

So I tell anybody, "Give your product away for a little bit. Try that, and see what happens. You'll find people who like your product, and if you're doing a good job, they'll eventually pay you to run your service."

TAKEAWAYS

⊰ In selling a new product or service, especially when you are selling an idea that flies in the face of conventional

wisdom, be prepared to hear "No"
repeatedly.

⚜ Consider giving away the product or
service for free at first. Use this as a
case study to learn how to make your
product or service work for a client.

⚜ In doing so you will find the people
who like your product and will pay you
for it.

Sell to the Organization, Not to the Individual

Charles Brewer

Executive Vice President,
U.S. Air Products and Services, DHL

Making the Sale

THE MOST COMMON MISTAKE people make with regard to negotiation—and I've made it many times myself, and certainly in the earlier days—is focusing in on one person. Certainly, as you get to the more complex sales, the number of stakeholders involved in a decision-making process widens, and it's highly unlikely that one person's going to take that risk on their shoulders on their own. In my opinion, and certainly in the industry I'm in, I've seen far too often where salespeople tend to focus in on the individual and don't think about the collective solution.

To give an example, about three or four years ago we were working with one of the world's largest retailers, which had a very large spend. We'd been working on them for many, many months—in fact, probably a couple of years—in terms of trying to convert them across to our organization. And in the one or two years prior to being successful, where I think we'd perhaps gone wrong was in focusing just on an individual's needs and

concerns around what we were trying to do
from a supply-chain perspective.

The tipping point came when we spent a
little bit of time actually sitting and thinking, rather than doing: what was the whole
makeup of that retail organization? What
was their raison d'être? What were they trying to establish in the marketplace? It wasn't
transportation. That's not what business
they were in; they were in retail.

Very quickly, we understood that there
were probably more than two or three people involved in the decision-making
process—and much more importantly, people who weren't involved in the decision
process but clearly had value to be gained
from perhaps the solution we were going to
present and would therefore influence that
group of people that was going to make a
decision. [They] were the ones where we
spent more of our time.

In this particular scenario, when we
looked at what that organization did—what
its mantra to its customers was—it was all

about customer service, the customer experience. That's how they have positioned themselves in the marketplace; that's how they have differentiated their store versus anybody else's store. And given that we had spent two years talking to the logistics organization and procurement, if you were sitting as CEO of that organization, you probably didn't spend an awful lot of time working out how procurement sits within the customer experience environment. But you did spend an awful lot of time with your customer service team. That's where the rubber hits the road as to what they were trying to deliver from a product position.

Having worked that out, we then spent a fair amount of time actually with the customer service department and working out what sort of pain points they were experiencing through transportation, because transportation is how they get their product to their customers. Clearly, it's an absolutely strategic imperative in terms of what their business model is. But no one had sat down with that customer service business

Making the Sale

unit and said, "What is it you really want? What are your pain points? How does transportation get in your way or help you?"

That took us about two or three months, working with the customer service group, to understand all those various elements. Having worked that out, we then moved on to the marketing function, went to the finance function, and literally went round the whole organization, looking at how supply chain, or transportation, impacted and affected them.

When we went back to the procurement and logistics group and showed them what we'd learned about their organization from the many other stakeholders, suddenly it was a very different discussion. It was no longer about price and commodity; it was about value and solution, which is the perfect place for a salesperson to be. And having worked on this business for two years, within two months we converted it to our organization—a very large sale.

It taught me very early on that in the larger, more complex sale, it's not one, two,

three, four, five people. It taught me to
map out the various people in the organization who would have a major influence or a
major impact on the decision, and who
was the recipient of the solution we were
presenting.

If you model the requirements [...],
what they're trying to achieve from a
transportational supply chain, from your
product, what they're trying to get out of
it, what the value is they can extract—and
it's the smallest thing sometimes, the most
bizarre things that perhaps you initially
wouldn't find—then you're in a far better
position to present an overall solution that
has an all-encompassing outcome to the
organization.

TAKEAWAYS

- ⚷ When negotiating a sale, don't focus on only one person. It's rare that a single individual has the sole decision-making power.

- ⚷ Take the time to identify the various parties who have influence on the decision and find out what their problems are.

- ⚷ Present a comprehensive solution that has an all-encompassing outcome for the organization.

—◆—

Selling Products to Your Sales Team

—◆—

Liam McGee

President, Global Consumer and Small Business Banking, Bank of America

IT'S MUCH SIMPLER to ask your teammates to build relationships with customers,
sell another product, if your teammates believe that they have the best product. If the
teammate has confidence that what they're

asking [customers] to consider is in their best interest—best price, best features, most reliable, going to make your life simple, whatever—our teammates in our experience will far exceed any sales goals we give them.

Where we've had challenges is where they may not necessarily believe that, and then you get down to what a lot of [salespeople] do: "I'm going to do this just because I have to." We have to understand what customers want, but we also have to understand what our associates want for their customers. So No Fee Mortgage PLUS, Keep the Change, SiteKey, and $0 online equity trades have all been things that have been good for customers but have also given our teammates a sense of pride, where they are much less reticent to ask you about that product, to recommend it to you, because they believe it's the best.

You can have the best sales incentives, best sales management process, but if your teammates believe that they're doing a good thing for the customer, at least in our company they will far exceed anything we ask them to do. If they don't, they'll meet what we ask them, but they won't do much more than that because they want to do the right thing for the customer. Our product manufacturers, our product groups, are having a greater appreciation for the importance of understanding the customer and the associate.

I can recall conversations a couple of years ago where the mortgage products managers would come to me and say, "We need to do this because this is what the customers want." And my response to them was, "I think it's important to understand that, and you can have the best product that you think responds to the voice of the customer, but if your teammates don't think it's the best product, they're not going to sell it."

In the mortgage business, that was a breakthrough. It took a couple of those conversations, because it was uncomfortable for me to say, "Hey, I understand you're responding to the voice of the customer, and I don't want to minimize that, but in this product in particular, especially if you want to sell it to the branches—because it's very complicated, and it takes a lot of time, and they don't want to be embarrassed, and they don't want to feel inadequate—then you'd better spend equal, if not more, time on what the associates want. What will they feel proud to sell to their customers? Because if you answer that question, they will literally talk to every customer in the bank about needing to have this product."

Out of that came a paradigm shift for us, and we're doing more of that in all of our other products around customers and associates: put the voices, those two voices, together. But I think in our company, to be honest with you, it may be more important that we give the associates what they feel proud of, even if it's a little less than what the customer wants, because our associates are so passionate that they will get their customers to understand the merits of the product. Even if it's compared with the best product ever but our associates don't think so, it may sit on the shelf.

TAKEAWAYS

- When selling, make sure that your salespeople believe they have the best product.

- Salespeople want to do what's right for the customer and will often exceed goals when they believe in the product.

- Spend equal if not more time with your salespeople than with your customers. Find out what your salespeople want and will feel proud to sell.

Winning New Business in the Service Industry

David Bell

Chairman Emeritus, Interpublic Group

THE YEAR IS 2001. The opportunity for the Interpublic Group is huge. The opportunity is that an $11 million revenue client, Bank of America, has decided to move from hundreds of suppliers—in every

field from sports marketing, direct response, interactive, experiential branding,
all the fields—to one.

The competition is very clear; it's all the
big holding companies. Omnicom [Group]
is clearly in a wonderful position. They
have one of their great providers deeply
entrenched in the client. The client has ac-
cepted the changes they need to, strategi-
cally, to make the change. They're looking
for what used to be called integrated marketing. They're also looking, as you might
imagine, for cost savings, but they're really
looking for what all clients are looking for.
They're looking for a chance in their process—and this applies to any professional
service—to understand what it would be like
to work with the company.

Omnicom makes a fatal strategic mistake;
they put in charge of their presentation a
silo head—an individual company head—
whose job it is to somehow rise above his
own silo and put together all of the rest of
the companies. Interpublic made one great

strategic decision, which was to anoint an
agnostic leader, beholden to no silo, and to
spend enough time with what turned out to
be sixteen different companies, working together in preparation for the pitch. Then
instead of the client listening to capabilities,
instead of the client seeing puppets jumping
up and down—I'm in charge of tax; I'm in
charge of this; or whatever the service might
be—they *felt* it. They felt that there was a
team that was cohesive. They felt that there
was a team that had a leader. They felt that
they would not need to manage individual
silos and that holism would be accomplished
because of what they saw and felt.

I think what's important here is that in
selling any professional service you must
not talk about capabilities; you must be what
you purport to be, and you must give the
prospect, or the client, a sense of feeling
what it would be like to work with you, a
sense of feeling what it would be like to sit in
a meeting and experience a team attacking
an issue, a problem, or an opportunity.

Making the Sale

I've thought about that lesson many,
many times. I think about it when I interview accounting firms. I think about it when
I interview real estate firms. In any professional service firm, if you are the buyer,
what you're really buying is, yes, credentials—are they big enough? Have they done
it before? Can they do it? But that's kind of
a given; that's table stakes. The differentiator is, would I look forward to a meeting
with them knowing that together we would
create something special? Would I look forward to a meeting feeling that they would
bring something to the table that would be
special?

Creating that sense in a credentials presentation is essential. That's the strategic lesson that I learned. We won [the Bank of
America project] hands down; and we won,
basically, hands down because we created an
experience that was powerful instead of a
meeting that was [only about] credentials.

TAKEAWAYS

⊰ When you're pitching new business, put together a team that focuses on experiences rather than credentials.

⊰ Share with the client what it would be like to work together. Give the client a sense of what it would be like to sit in meetings or tackle tough issues with you and your team.

⊰ The true differentiator in winning business is whether you bring something special to the table.

Sales Leadership Is Not a Spectator Sport

Doug Elix

Senior Vice President and Group Executive,
Sales and Distribution, IBM

THE MOST INTERESTING STORY I have around developing one of my sales leaders is when we were jointly working on a major engagement with a big client in New York City. I had found out [that the

agreement] had actually stalled, and un-
known to my sales leader, I had found this
out from one of his team [members], who
had actually come around the side and told
me that the sale had stalled.

I arranged to go and call with my sales
leader on the client, to find out what had
happened and to try and get it back on
track. We explored it, and we found out exactly what we weren't doing correctly and
why we were not satisfying the client need.
After a long conversation, we got the sale
back on track. We were feeling pretty good
about ourselves, and we walked outside. We
debriefed outside the building on what to
do next. Then we all started going off to our
cars. My sales leader went off to his car, and
I said, "Where are you going?"

He said, "I'm going back to the office."

I said, "You being in the office was what
caused this problem in the first place. You
should go back in the building, and until
you get this thing finished, you should stay
with the client." And literally he did not go

back into the office for two weeks, until he finished the job.

To me it was a very interesting experience about sales leadership. To me the lesson learned is, sales leadership is not a spectator sport; you have to participate, you have to be personally involved in it. It's not about sitting in the office or sticking to a process or presiding over your salespeople. It's all about active coaching, active participation. And it is a discipline; it's not an art. You have to be involved. You have to know whether you're meeting client needs. You have to have compelling value propositions. You have to use consultative selling. And you have to have a will to close and finish the work.

Lesson number one: no matter how high you get in the organization, always make time to go out and participate in these engagements with your people so that you can actually lead by example and can coach on the job. The second lesson is to constantly review with my sales leaders where they are in the progression, especially of their major sales, so that I can listen and, from my experience, give them advice on how they can improve on that. To me it's a matter of personal involvement.

TAKEAWAYS

⇥ Sales leadership is an area in which you must participate and be personally involved.

⇥ No matter how high your position, you have to get out of the office and coach by example.

⇥ Meet with your sales team and share your experiences as a way to help them improve.

The Case Against Rank Ordering Your Sales Team

Andris Zoltners

Founder, ZS Associates

A NUMBER OF YEARS AGO, we were thinking about performance management within my consulting firm. There were a number of people at the principal level who were on a committee to look at this, who

Making the Sale

were suggesting that what we should do is
look at all our managers; we should rank
order them on some important metrics. At
that time, I was kind of against it, and I ar-
gued against it. We didn't do it. The pro-
posal there was that we rank order people,
and we'd tell them where they were in the
rank ordering.

What was interesting was that within six
months to a year, I was in an executive class.
The whole question of rank ordering came
up, and here's what very many companies
were doing. They were taking all their salespeople on important metrics—like sales,
percent growth attainment, growth over last
year—they were ranking these individuals,
and they were publishing it. Everyone in the
sales force could see where they were; they
could see where everybody else was. This was
a group of individuals in an executive semi-
nar who were arguing this way. I remem-
bered from my own firm arguing the other
way, so I wanted to know the reasons.

It was very uniform, and [it was the same]
discussion I've had with many executive

groups subsequently. Here's what they're saying: sales is a competitive space; we're all very competitive people; we like to know how we're doing, and it's very motivating.

In fact, I can tell you about a person who, in a hundred-person sales force, was eighty-seventh and moved up to thirtieth. We always have these heroes in mind and these success stories. Well, of course, as that person was moving up, understand other people were moving down. This is the theory behind it. Competitive people . . . You look at football rankings, you look at baseball rankings, you see all the teams, and you see where they are. Sales is like that.

The question I began to ask these classes was the following: take that same hundred-person sales force, and let's rank all the individuals. Now, see yourself within that ranking. Where would you be as you start going down? At what point do you start feeling unsuccessful? People start reacting to that. And what you begin to see is people say, "Number 2"—well, that's certainly a little bold. But [I could be in the] top 5 percent, top 10 percent. The moment I fall out of the President's Club I don't feel successful.

Probably the lowest you'll see anybody go is 50 percent. So here's the question. If 50 percent is the cutoff, do you want half of your sales force to feel unsuccessful? Is that the message you want to give your people, so that they walk around with a cloud over their heads like Charlie Brown? Is that what you really want with your sales force?

People began to ponder this. And the discovery was, probably not. All of a sudden, this force ranking becomes a wall of shame. And then you start asking yourself, "What? Why is it that managers would allow this wall of shame?"

Here's a theory for you: I think managers frequently abdicate managerial courage by putting together that kind of list, because they don't have to tell the people how they're doing. Rank ordering does it for them. It's a management tool to give people bad news. Who wants to give people bad news? No one wants to do that, right? So I'm using this tool now to give people bad news.

Making the Sale

The bottom line on this, in my opinion, here is a better practice: if you want competitiveness—and not just to highlight the top performers—let the top performers feel great. It's like pro ball. Let's highlight those people, show other individuals what it takes to be within that set, highlight the heroes. And with the other individuals, it's the manager's job. The manager has to go and tell those individuals where they are in the ranking and help them move up. No one else has to know that you're eighty-seventh in the sales force; it's just between you and your manager.

To me, that's the best practice. If you want to publish something, publish the top ones. Manage the other ones for performance.

TAKEAWAYS

- Rank ordering is frequently seen as an important tool because it breeds competition among motivated sales staff.

- However, not everyone can rank number 1. That's when rank ordering can actually become a "wall of shame."

- A better practice is to showcase top performers as a goal to be achieved and to use rankings as a tool to manage performance privately.

Building a High-Performing Sales Team

Robert Malcolm

President, Global Marketing, Sales, and Innovation, Diageo

IN ALL OF MY YEARS in marketing, and then quite a few years in general management, there were a few tricks, or a few principles, that seemed to work in building high-performing sales teams. Probably my best example of that is when I was in the Middle East with Procter & Gamble in the early nineties. I was running eight countries in the Middle East. This was an organization where we were selling [Procter & Gamble products] through distributors throughout the region to consumers in eight or nine different markets.

The situation that I walked into was a relatively low-performing sales organization, because it was selling through distributors and wholesalers. It was very good at finding ways to load up the distributors and wholesalers. The result of that was, we weren't winning at the retail outlets because we were concentrating on the wholesale outlets.

The first thing that I had to do was to change the focus of where our sales organization spent its time, focusing on winning at retail. I had to find a sales leader who was up for that task and up for the change that was required in the sales organization to do that. So I replaced the sales leader and found someone who was capable of doing that.

The second thing was to change the culture and get the culture focused on a new definition of winning. Not simply winning by selling more and making the annual sales quota—because with the looseness of the wholesalers in the Middle East that was relatively easy to do—but to actually get them focused on winning at the retail coalface, up against our competitor. So the goals were winning the distribution game, winning the shelving game, and building share.

The third thing I had to do was get the rewards right, to reward the kind of behavior that you want [in order] to develop a winning sales organization.

Then, last but not least—and this has been something that's been a hallmark of mine, in any general management, marketing, or sales leadership role I've ever had—was to live with the sales guys, out in the field. Work with them. I would spend one day every week in the field with my sales organization so I knew what was going on. I wasn't getting it from sales reports—although I was getting the data, of course—but I was in every corner of Saudi Arabia, Bahrain, and Kuwait seeing what was going on, talking with wholesalers. I knew when the wholesalers were being stuffed, and I knew when we weren't winning at retail.

Making the Sale

There's one anecdote that I think illustrates what it felt like. One day, I was in the eastern province of Saudi Arabia, in Dammam and Al-Khobar, and I was working with the unit manager in that region, calling on stores. I observed that there was someone going in and out of all the little retail outlets just in front of us. He had a white van, and he was taking product in and out. When we got there, what we discovered was that the retailer didn't actually have any money left to buy our products. After about the third time, I asked my unit manager, who spoke Arabic—I didn't speak Arabic at the time—to find out what was going on.

We discovered this person was an independent van salesman—an entrepreneur, if you will. With his own van, he'd go to the wholesale market and load it up with the product that he thought the stores needed. He'd walk into the stores, he'd ask the store clerk—never the owner, the store clerk—how much money he had in the cash drawer. The store clerk would open up the cash drawer and tell him. He'd then take 80 percent of that money and fill up the store with what-

ever the person needed—with 80 percent of
that money—and walk out.

I thought that was a fantastic way of selling
and meeting the local customer needs. We
stopped the guy, got in front of him at the
next account, and offered him a job at
P&G. He became our first van salesman in
the eastern province. Through him, we
found nine others just like him, and we
built an independent van sales network, all
of whom knew the retail outlets.

The result of that was, we absolutely
crushed the competition in all of those small
outlets, through that very different approach
to selling. The secret to discovering that was,
I was in the field regularly observing, seeing
what was going on. It was very real.

The business results that we got in Saudi
Arabia were very, very strong. We had strong
market shares to start with, but during the
period I was there, as we built the sales force
capability, we generated record market
shares in every single category that we were
doing business in.

The thing I probably take the most pride
in is when I left Saudi Arabia, about 1995,

and the sales force took me out to dinner. They gave me a gorgeous silver plate, with an outline of my Middle East assignment in it, which said, "From a sales force that loves the attention."

TAKEAWAYS

- To build a high-performing sales team, you need to focus where the salespeople are spending their time, set up the right culture, and provide the right rewards.

- As a sales leader, you must spend time in the field, working with the sales staff and meeting with customers.

- Being in the field helps you to better meet customer needs and to realize opportunities you would otherwise never encounter.

David Balter is founder and CEO of the word-of-mouth marketing and media company BzzAgent.

Mr. Balter founded BzzAgent in 2002. Since that time, his company has provided word-of-mouth media services for dozens of *Fortune* 500 companies and has been featured in the *New York Times Sunday Magazine,* the *Wall Street Journal,* and the *Economist,* and on National Public Radio.

A cofounder and current board member of the Word of Mouth Marketing Association, Mr. Balter is an international speaker on the topic of word-of-mouth marketing. He has presented for corporations, associations, and nonprofit groups throughout the United States, Europe, and Asia. He is the coauthor of *Grapevine: The New Art of Word-of-Mouth Marketing,* which has become one of the industry's most recognized business titles.

Dubbed a "serial entrepreneur" by *Boston Globe,* Mr. Balter built and sold two promotional agencies before forming BzzAgent. He was named to the "40 Under 40" list by *Boston Business Journal* in 2006 as well as by Advertising Specialty Institute in 2001.

About the Contributors

David Bell is Chairman Emeritus of Interpublic Group, a global advertising and marketing services company, a position he has held since 2005.

Previously, Mr. Bell was President and CEO of Bozell Worldwide. He started at Bozell in 1975 when the agency acquired Knox Reeves Advertising, where he had been President since 1972. Mr. Bell then served as Chairman and CEO of True North Communications, Inc.

In 2001 Mr. Bell joined the Interpublic Group of Companies, Inc. as Vice Chairman, and he served as CEO from 2003 to 2005.

In addition, Mr. Bell became a director of the Ad Council in 1997 and served as its Chairman from June 2002 until May 2003. He also served as Chairman of the American Association of Advertising Agencies in 1996–1997 and was a two-time Chairman of the American Advertising Federation. He is currently Chairman Emeritus of the Advertising Educational Foundation and Ad Council. He is a director of PRO-AD PAC, the industry's political action committee, and Primedia, Inc., and is director for Warnaco Group, Inc.

Charles Brewer is Executive Vice President, U.S. Air Products and Services, for DHL International GmbH, an express delivery and logistics company.

Before his appointment as Executive Vice President, Mr. Brewer managed country operations in Malaysia. He has more than twenty-one years of industry experience at DHL. Before his posting in

About the Contributors

Malaysia, he held senior positions in Asia Pacific and the United Kingdom.

Doug Elix is Senior Vice President & Group Executive, Sales and Distribution, of IBM (International Business Machines, Corp.), a top producer of computer products and services.

Mr. Elix began his career with IBM in 1969. In 1990, he was named Director of the Finance Industry for IBM Asia Pacific, in 1991 he became Director of Operations for IBM Australia, and in 1994 he became CEO for IBM Australia.

In 1996 he was appointed President and CEO of Integrated Systems Solutions Corp. (ISSC), a wholly owned services subsidiary of IBM, until becoming General Manager of IBM Global Services, North America. In 1998 he became General Manager of IBM Global Services, Americas.

Mr. Elix began his current position in May 2004, after serving as Senior Vice President & Group Executive for IBM Global Services beginning in October 1999.

In addition, Mr. Elix serves as director for Royal Bank of Canada.

Sir Richard Evans is Chairman of United Utilities, a position he has held since 2001.

Sir Richard started his career at the Ministry of Transport and Civil Aviation. He joined the British Aircraft Corporation (BAC) and was promoted to Commercial Director of the Warton Division of British Aerospace (BAe) in 1978.

About the Contributors

In 1981, he became Deputy Managing Director for BAe Warton. Three years later he was made Deputy Managing Director of the British Aerospace Military Aircraft Division. A year later he was appointed to the board of British Aerospace as Marketing Director, and the following year became Chairman of the British Aerospace Defense companies.

Sir Richard was appointed CEO of British Aerospace in 1990. In 1998 he joined British Aerospace as Chairman, and he continued to chair the company when it became BAE Systems following the merger with Marconi Electronic Systems. In July 2004 he retired from the board but continues to advise the company.

In 1997 he joined the board of United Utilities, Plc as a director and was appointed Chairman four years later.

Mel Lagomasino is CEO of GenSpring Family Offices, LLC, formerly Asset Management Advisors, LLC, a multifamily office that provides independent advice to families of substantial wealth.

Before joining AMA in November 2005, Ms. Lagomasino was chairman and CEO of JP Morgan Private Bank (part of JPMorgan Chase & Co.), one of the largest providers of wealth management services worldwide, with more than $300 billion in client assets and more than $1.5 billion in revenues.

Ms. Lagomasino's career with J.P. Morgan began when she joined The Chase Manhattan Corporation in 1983 as Vice President and Team Leader for Latin America.

About the Contributors

In 1989 she was named head of the Private Bank Western Hemisphere Area. She became the Global Private Bank executive in 1997, in charge of Chase's worldwide private banking business. Before joining Chase, she was a vice president at Citibank, and before that worked at the United Nations.

Ms. Lagomasino was on the board of directors of The Coca-Cola Company and is a director of Avon Products, Inc., and Lincoln Center Theater. She is a trustee of the Synergos Institute and a member of the Council on Foreign Relations and The Economic Club of New York.

Robert Malcolm is President of Global Marketing, Sales, and Innovation for Diageo, Plc. He has held this position since September 2000.

Before joining Diageo, Mr. Malcolm served as Scotch Category Director and then Global Marketing Director with United Distillers & Vintners. He also held various marketing and general management positions with The Procter & Gamble Company.

Since June 2007, Mr. Malcolm has also served as director of Logitech, Inc., a manufacturer of computer control devices.

Liam McGee is President of Global Consumer and Small Business Banking at Bank of America.

McGee joined Bank of America in 1990 and has broad leadership experience in consumer and commercial banking, as well as technology and operations. He led the California Consumer Bank and Corporate Technology and Operations before he

was named President, Bank of America California.
McGee is a member of the National Urban League
Board of Trustees and the Arts & Science Council
Board of Directors in Charlotte, North Carolina.
He has also served as Chairman of the University of
San Diego Board of Trustees and the United Way of
Greater Los Angeles, and two terms as a director of
the Federal Reserve Bank of San Francisco.

Sir David Michels is former Group Chief Executive of Hilton Hotels Corp., a position he left in
2006. Currently, he is Group Chief Executive for
Scandic Hotels AB.

In 1981 Sir David joined Ladbroke Group, Plc as
Sales and Marketing Director of Ladbroke Hotels.
He then became Managing Director of Ladbroke's
Leisure Division in 1983, becoming Managing Di-
rector of Ladbroke Hotels in 1985.

He spent fifteen years with Grand Metropolitan
Hotels, Plc, mainly in sales and marketing, which
culminated in a board position as Worldwide Marketing Director.

Following Ladbroke Group's acquisition of Hil-
ton International in 1987, Sir David became Hilton's
Senior Vice President, Sales and Marketing. In
1989 he moved up to become Deputy Chairman of
Hilton UK, and Executive Vice President, Hilton
International.

He joined Stakis as CEO in 1991. Eight years
later the company was acquired by Hilton Group for
around £1.2 billion. He joined Hilton International
as CEO in April 1999 and became group CEO of

About the Contributors

the Hilton Group (formerly Ladbroke Group) in June 2000. He left the company in 2006.

Sir David is also a director of British Land Company, Plc; EasyJet Airline Company Ltd.; Marks & Spencer, Plc; and Strategic Hotels & Resorts, Inc. In 2006 he received the International Hotel Investment Forum's Lifetime Achievement Award.

Gill Rider is Director General, Leadership and People Strategy, at the Cabinet Office (United Kingdom).

Ms. Rider started her career in the financial markets, healthcare, and government industries. She also worked in the customer service area examining industry best practices.

She joined Accenture in 1979 and became a partner in 1990. With operational responsibility for Accenture's Utilities practice in Europe and South Africa, she also served as Chairman of Accenture's United Kingdom and Ireland geographic unit. She then headed the European and Latin American operations of Accenture's Resources operating unit.

Ms. Rider became Accenture's Chief Leadership Officer when the position was created in March 2002. She headed the company's Organization and Leadership Development group and was responsible for developing the leadership capabilities and professional skills of Accenture's people and fostering a culture that encourages diversity and achievement.

She was appointed Director General, Leadership and People Strategy, at the Cabinet Office in February 2006. In this role Ms. Rider helps to

About the Contributors

drive strategic change within the civil service as it undertakes programs of major reform. This includes providing leadership for the service's programs transforming the professional skills of civil servants, developing leaders, and promoting diversity.

She will also act as Head of Profession for HR professionals across government, thereby building up the service's HR capability.

In 2006 Ms. Rider became a director for De La Rue, Plc, the world's largest commercial security printer and papermaker.

Richard T. Santulli is founder and CEO of NetJets Inc., the company that has revolutionized private and corporate business jet travel through fractional aircraft ownership.

From 1969 to 1979, Mr. Santulli was an investment banker with Goldman, Sachs & Co., where he held various managerial positions, including Vice President of Investment Banking and President of Goldman Sachs Leasing Corporation.

In 1986, he developed the successful NetJets program. In 1996, he introduced the NetJets Europe program, and in 1999 he inaugurated NetJets Middle East. Mr. Santulli has plans to expand the NetJets fractional aircraft ownership program into South America and the Asia/Pacific countries to provide a worldwide network of NetJets aircraft.

Mr. Santulli is also director of the Andre Agassi Charitable Foundation.

About the Contributors

Phil Smith is Head of Technology & Corporate Marketing, Europe, for Cisco Systems, Inc. Cisco Systems is a leader in hardware, software, and service offerings used to create Internet solutions.

Mr. Smith's career path includes working for IBM and Philips (Koninklijke Philips Electronics N.V.) in various senior roles, including design and implementation of some of today's largest networks. Before joining Cisco, he spent five years at Pipex Internet Limited (now part of UUNET's global Internet service provider business, a brand of Verizon Communications, Inc.), the first commercial ISP in the United Kingdom.

Mr. Smith joined Cisco in 1994 in a technical consulting role. He was formerly Business Development Director for Cisco UK and Ireland, where he was responsible for market development, technical strategy, and alliances. He also drives Cisco's local investment and acquisition activities.

Mr. Smith is a frequent public speaker on Internet, e-business, and strategy issues and is a regular correspondent on the expert panel in the *Sunday Times* "Enterprise Network" feature.

William Ury is the Director of the Global Negotiation Project (GNP), formerly the Nuclear Negotiation Project and Project on Preventing War, at Harvard Law School.

Mr. Ury earned his BA from Yale and his PhD, in social anthropology, from Harvard. He has conducted research in corporate boardrooms and other locations throughout the world.

Mr. Ury is the cofounder of Harvard Law School's Program on Negotiation. His research focuses on the global dynamics of transforming destructive conflicts into constructive processes. As one of the world's foremost experts in negotiation, he has mediated everything from corporate mergers to sensitive political issues. He has served as a consultant to many of the biggest U.S. corporations, including AT&T, IBM, and Ford Motor Company, as well as to the Pentagon and the White House.

He also cofounded the International Negotiation Network, which is chaired by President Jimmy Carter, and he remains an adviser. The organization seeks to end civil wars around the world.

Mr. Ury is the coauthor of the bestselling book *Getting to Yes* and the author of *Getting Past No*.

Andris Zoltners is the founder of ZS Associates, Inc., a global sales and marketing consulting firm. Founded in 1983, ZS focuses on matters ranging from go-to-market strategy and sales force design to areas of implementation such as compensation and account targeting.

In addition, Mr. Zoltners is a professor of marketing at the Kellogg School of Management at Northwestern University, where he has been a member of the faculty for more than thirty years. Before this, he was a member of the Business School faculty at the University of Massachusetts.

⊰ ACKNOWLEDGMENTS ⊱

First and foremost, a heartfelt thanks goes to all of the executives who have candidly shared their hard-earned experience and battle-tested insights for the Lessons Learned series.

Angelia Herrin at Harvard Business School Publishing consistently offered un-wavering support, good humor, and counsel from the inception of this ambitious project.

Brian Surette, Hollis Heimbouch, and David Goehring provided invaluable editorial direction, perspective, and encouragement. Much appreciation goes to Jennifer Lynn for her research and diligent attention to detail. Many thanks to the entire HBSP team of designers, copy editors, and marketing professionals who helped bring this series to life.

Finally, thanks to our fellow cofounder James MacKinnon and the entire Fifty

Acknowledgments

Lessons team for the tremendous amount of time, effort, and steadfast support for this project.

—Adam Sodowick
    Andy Hasoon
    Directors and Cofounders
    Fifty Lessons